ketogenic diet
FROZEN
DESSERTS

OVER 30 DECADENT, **LOW CARB HIGH FAT** HOMEMADE ICE CREAM
AND FROZEN TREATS RECIPES

Published by The Fruitful Mind

www.fruitfulbooks.com

Disclaimer

Table of Contents

Introduction 5

Simple Keto Diet Guidelines 8

A Few Words About the Ingredients 16

Rich and Luscious Ice Creams 25
Blueberry Buckle Ice Cream............................... 26
Browned Butter and Pecan Ice Cream.............. 29
Maple and Buttered Coconut Ice Cream............ 32
Raspberry Almond Cheesecake Ice Cream....... 34
Ultimate Vanilla Ice Cream 36
Pumpkin Pie Ice Cream....................................... 39
Lemon Poppy Seed Ice Cream............................. 41
Mojito Ice Cream 43
Chocolate Pistachio Ice Cream 45
Extra Creamy Hazelnut Coffee Ice Cream 47

Frozen Treats on a Stick.............................49
Strawberry Lime Popsicles................................. 50
Orange Creamsicles... 52
Minty Cantaloupe Pops 54
Raspberry Forest Bars 56
Spicy Peach Layer Bars 58
Creamy Fudgesicles... 61
Raspberry Latte Bars.. 63
Creamy Peanut Butter Popsicles 65
Cannoli Popsicles 67
Cranberry Hazelnut Power Pops 69

Keto Frozen Pies 71
Strawberry and Peaches Pie 72
Death by Chocolate Pie....................................... 75
Coconut Blackberry Fluff Pie 78
Better Than a PB&J Sandwich Pie 81

Keto Frozen Dessert Bombs 85
   Coconut Lime Bombs 86
   Blackberry Coconut Cheesecake Bombs 88
   Walnut Orange Bombs 90
   Blueberry Basil Bombs 92
   Italian Dessert Bombs 94
   Minty Chocolate Bombs 96
   Butter Rum Bombs 98
   Decadent Salted Double Chocolate Bombs..... 100
   Maple Nut Bombs 102

Conclusion 104

Introduction

There are few things more satisfying and rewarding than the cool creaminess of a luscious frozen dessert. You know, the kind that melts in your mouth and spreads the sweet flavors over each of your taste buds. Perfect for a warm summer day, a celebration or just because, ice cream and frozen desserts are the quintessential dessert. The only problem is that because of their high fat and sugar content, many desserts, especially rich, creamy ones, have developed a bad reputation with those that strive to live a healthy lifestyle. How many times have you craved something sweet, but told yourself no, simply because it seemed like a poor dietary choice? This idea becomes even more amplified if you have committed yourself to a dietary plan. It seems every sweet treat is the end of your diet just waiting to happen.

Lucky for you, eating ketogenically means that you do not have to forgo one delicious bite of sweetness. Ketogenic eating is a dietary style that focuses both on low carbohydrates and high fats, with moderate amounts of protein. Your first image of this might be a plate overfilled with meats and cheeses and you might think that there is nothing dessert like about it. However, the keto diet actually provides the perfect canvas for rich, creamy desserts. A combination of high fat dairy, rich creamy cheeses and silky fats like coconut oil and full cream butter come together with an amazing variety of flavors and other ingredients to produce deserts that are so rich and so decadent that it seems impossible to be able to enjoy them while on a "diet".

However, eating ketogenically isn't really a diet at all, but instead a lifestyle. And why would you commit to a lifestyle where you never got to enjoy the sweeter things in life? This book is full of recipes that will help you do just that, enjoy the sweetness of natural and healthy ketogenic eating. Frozen desserts are not only among the most favored, but they are also the easiest to prepare and generally require few ingredients.

You can make them as simple or elaborate as you want, and each one will be equally delicious. Most of the recipes in this book require just a few minutes of time to prepare and then your freezer or ice cream maker takes care of the rest.

You can eat ketogenically and have your dessert too. Enjoy!

Simple Keto Diet Guidelines

You probably already know the number one reason that diet plans fail. It is that people get bored and they miss favorite foods, such as desserts, which are often forbidden or at least extremely restricted. One of the best things about eating ketogenically is that so many of the treasured foods that are longed for on traditional low fat, low calorie diets are included in your daily eating plan, and you can enjoy them in abundance. A common misconception about ketogenic, or low carbohydrate eating in general, is that you miss out on dessert and other sweet treats, or if you are able to indulge you can only do so using unnatural sweeteners and other chemical produced low carb ingredients.

In this book, we have set forth to show you that you can eat naturally, and indulge your sweet tooth at the same time. However, to gain the most from your ketogenic eating plan it is important that you still stick to the ketogenic guidelines. You might already be familiar with what defines a ketogenic diet. If you are, then use this section as a quick reminder or reference if you have questions. If you are unsure about what defines ketogenic, read through this and keep in handy for times when you have questions or are unsure. Here are the basic ketogenic principals in a nutshell:

1. You do not need to count calories, unless you want to. The keto diet helps you lose weight by changing the way your body metabolizes food and burns fuel. When you enter ketosis, your body is not relying on recently consumed carbohydrates for fuel and instead digs deep into your fat reserves for the energy instead. The amount of calories you consume does not affect this, and only affects overall weight loss results for very few people. Still, you may be under a physician's advice or feel more comfortable restricting your calories. If this is true, keep in mind that a ketogenic diet is naturally higher in fat, and therefore higher in calories. This would make it difficult to adhere to any severe calorie restrictions.

2. Don't worry about overeating; your appetite will balance itself out. You might think during the initial stages of a ketogenic diet that you are eating too much, or consuming too many calories. It might seem impossible to you that you can carry on at this rate and still manage to lose weight. To this I say trust your body. After about two weeks, your appetite will naturally begin to diminish.

3. Ketogenic eating is about more than just eating low carb. Traditional low carb diets rely on a hefty portion of protein to balance out the lack of carbs. The ketogenic diet includes protein, but the emphasis is on calories from fat. For the most natural and healthiest keto diet possible, stick to natural sources of fats that also deliver additional nutritional benefits. Choose olive oil, avocado oil, coconut oil, and full fat creamy butter instead of vegetable oil, canola oil or margarine.

4. Do not reach for lower fat substitutes. Stick to full fat dairy, and even though lean healthy proteins are great, it is absolutely fine to indulge in protein that is a little richer in fat content. Choose heavy cream or milk because even whole vitamin D milk still has too much sugar for a ketogenic diet and can interfere with ketosis and blood sugar levels.

5. Be careful of artificial sweeteners. You do have to limit, or completely eliminate if necessary, items such as regular table sugar, brown sugar, honey and syrups. You can choose sugar free sweeteners, or ingredients created to be sugar free with low carbohydrates, but it is still best to stick to sweeteners that are naturally derived. Erythritol is a natural sugar alcohol and stevia is a naturally derived sweetener. Both of these options are natural, have no negative side effects and contain zero carbohydrates.

6. The magic ration that you want to aim for is to 70-20-10. That is seventy percent of your calories coming from fat sources, twenty percent of your calories coming from protein sources and ten percent of your calories coming from carbohydrates. Aiming for this number doesn't mean that you are going to fail if you don't hit it exactly. It is more of a reminder that you need to focus a high percentage of your calories on fats and the lowest amounts on carbohydrates.

7. You might choose to keep track of calories, you might choose to keep track of grams of fats, protein and carbohydrates, or you might choose to eat intuitively according to the plan and not give calculations much thought at all. Do what works best for you and according to what provides you with the best results. If you do like to keep track of calories and where they are coming from remember that one gram of fat contains nine calories, one gram of protein contains four calories and one gram of carbohydrate contains four calories. So ten grams of fat will provide ninety calories, while ten grams of protein or carbohydrates would provide forty grams of carbohydrates each.

8. You might find it useful, especially in the beginning, to keep track of how many grams of carbohydrates you consume on a daily basis. Most people can reach and maintain ketosis somewhere between thirty and sixty grams of carbohydrates per day. This is actually quite a wide range and your individual physiology is going to determine where on the scale you need to be. In the beginning strive for 30-35 grams of carbohydrates per day and adjust as needed. Do not go below twenty grams of carbohydrates per day for any length of time. Consuming that few carbohydrates can actually be detrimental to your health, which is also counterproductive to your efforts.

9. Eat as often as you are hungry. You should consume at least three larger meals and several small snacks each day. You might be the type who likes a large, satisfying meal or you might prefer to graze on smaller amounts of food throughout the day. The main thing to remember is that you should not go more than three to four hours without eating. At that point, your blood sugar begins to plummet and you are more prone to side effects as well as temptations that might sabotage your efforts.

10. Eat sweets in moderation. This book is all about the sweeter side of ketogenic eating. The recipes are designed to fit within ketogenic guidelines. However, some recipes contain fruit or chocolate, which in small amounts are just fine, but if you overindulge it can cause real problems for your progress. Additionally, you should be getting your energy and calories from a variety of sources.

11. Enjoy every minute of your ketogenic lifestyle. Once you really understand what it means to eat ketogenically, the culinary world that is open to you is both vast and exciting.

A Few Words About the Ingredients

Satisfying your sweet tooth while eating ketogenically is actually quite simple with just a few ingredients on hand. Most of the ingredients that you will find in these recipes are not only familiar, but very likely to already be on your list of kitchen staples. Just to make sure that you are familiar with all of them, we have included a list of some must haves for keto sweet treats.

Sweeteners

Erythritol:

This is a sugar alcohol that has zero calories or carbohydrates. It rates a zero on the glycemic index and has zero effect on blood sugar. Erythritol can be found in both granulated and powdered forms as a replacement for table sugar.

Stevia:

This is a natural sweetener that is a product of the stevia plant. As a replacement for table sugar, stevia has zero calories and is an appropriate choice for people who follow a low carbohydrate diet. If you are unfamiliar with stevia, it is actually much sweeter than sugar, and therefore you do not need as much. Stevia comes in liquid and powdered forms. The liquid form of stevia is the type used most frequently in the recipes in this book.

Fat Sources

Cocoa Butter:

This rich, creamy fat is the product of the cocoa bean. Many people thick of cocoa butter as only being used in skin care and cosmetic preparations, but cocoa butter is one of the primary ingredients in both white and milk chocolate. Cocoa butter can seem like both a liquid and a solid at room or body temperature, as illustrated by chocolate's melt in your mouth consistency. It makes a perfect fattening and emulsifying agent for creamy keto desserts.

Full Fat Coconut Milk:

This ingredient really is a simple as it sounds. You might notice when you go to purchase coconut milk that many options you find in the store have been altered to include flavor or to be reduced in calories. What you want is plain, pure coconut milk. The best way get the most creaminess from your coconut milk is to purchase cans of it and then place them, unopened, in the refrigerator overnight. This will cause a thick, fattier layer to form on top. Use just this in your recipes for extra creaminess.

Coconut Oil:

This creamy oil is solid at room temperature, but has a very low melting point. This makes it perfect for adding creamy consistency to frozen desserts that will melt creamily in your mouth. Coconut oil is known for its multitude of health benefits and should be in every keto pantry.

Heavy Whipping Cream:

Use heavy whipping cream in place of regular milk in all of your recipes. Milk is higher in sugar and lower in fat, meaning it can sneakily up your carbohydrate intake, spike your blood sugar and interfere with ketosis.

Creamy Cheeses:

Decedent, creamy cheeses such as mascarpone, ricotta and cream cheese are a ketogenic dream. These cheeses add flavor, texture, character and promote the higher fat ratio that is necessary in ketogenic eating.

Chocolate:

Just because you are eating ketogenically doesn't mean that you have to forgo your favorite chocolate. You can enjoy it, and you should. Just make sure that it is at least 70% pure cocoa and that any cocoa powder that you use is dark and unsweetened.

Extracts:

Extracts are your friend when it comes to adding in interesting flavors without adding a bunch of extra carbs. Choose from a wide range of flavors, or make your own. Extracts do have some carbohydrate value, but you use such a small amount that it is negated over the portion sizes.

Fruits

If ketogenic and fruit sound like opposites to you, you are not alone. Many people think that eating ketogenically means giving up on fruits for the long haul. The fact is that there are fruits that are relatively low in carbohydrates and can be enjoyed in moderation. It is best to pair these fruits with ample fats and proteins rather than eating them on their own. The top ten lowest carbohydrate fruits are:

• Citrus fruits such as lemon and limes
• Raspberries
• Blackberries
• Cranberries
• Blueberries
• Strawberries
• Watermelon
• Cantaloupe
• Peaches
• Papaya

You should avoid fruits with the highest amount of sugars such as: bananas, mangoes, grapes, figs, cherries and tangerines.

Creating Your Own Desserts

This book has been intended to provide you with delicious and satisfying sweet treats for you to enjoy while eating ketogenically. However, there will be times when you will want to extend beyond the recipes in this book and come up with something on your own. The good news is that developing your own keto friendly dessert recipes, especially of the frozen variety, is incredibly simple.

As a general rule, to create a frozen dessert you first want to take into consideration the consistency and texture that you are looking for. Higher fat liquids like heavy cream will make for the creamiest treats, and adding a creamy cheese will add richness and texture. Next, come up with any combination of keto friendly add ins including nuts, spices, sugar free flavorings, dark chocolate and fruit from the above provided list. Then form it into bombs, popsicle, ice cream or bars. It really is that simple. Don't feel confined by your ketogenic diet; instead let it inspire culinary creativity.

Rich and Luscious
ICE
CREAMS

The following recipes have been created for use with an ice cream maker. If you do not have one, there is no need to miss out on any of these delicious creations. To make these ice creams without an ice cream maker, simply pour the mixtures into a large pan and place in the freezer. Remove the ice cream from the freezer every 30-45 minutes and stir, or scrape, to promote a creamier consistency. As the ice cream begins to thicken and freeze you can even use an immersion blender to add a creamier, fluffier consistency. If there are any chunky add ins, save them for when the ice cream just begins to thicken and freeze. This will prevent the add ins from sinking to the bottom and not being evenly distributed throughout.

Blueberry Buckle Ice Cream

Serves: 6

Net Carbs: 4.9 g

Nutritional Information: Calories 223.8, Total Fat 20.8 g, Total Carbohydrate 14.5 g, Dietary Fiber 9.6 g, Sugars 2.9 g, Protein 4.0 g

Ingredients:

1 cup heavy cream

¼ cup erythritol

3 egg yolks

1 teaspoon vanilla extract

1 teaspoon cinnamon

¼ teaspoon xanthan gum

1 cup blueberries

½ cup almonds, chopped

Directions:

Place the heavy cream in a saucepan over low heat.

Once the cream has heated, add in the erythritol. Heat, stirring constantly until the erythritol has completely dissolved. Remove from heat.

Place the egg yolks in a bowl.

Take ¼ cup of the warm cream and slowly drizzle it into the eggs, while whisking constantly to temper the eggs so that they do not cook. Mix in the xanthan gum and cinnamon at this time as well.

Next, slowly add in the remaining creams into the eggs, stirring constantly until the mixture is creamy and a little frothy.

Stir in the blueberries and almonds. Add the mixture to an ice cream maker and follow the manufacturer's instructions.

Browned Butter and Pecan Ice Cream

Serves: 6

Net Carbs: 2.8 g

Nutritional Information: Calories 293.0, Total Fat 28.4 g, Total Carbohydrate 5.3 g, Dietary Fiber 2.5 g, Sugars 1.1 g, Protein 5.7 g

Ingredients:

¼ cup butter

1 cup pecans, chopped

½ teaspoon salt

½ cup ricotta cheese

½ cup cooked pumpkin

½ teaspoon cinnamon

½ teaspoon coriander

2 cups whole fat coconut milk

3 egg yolks

½ teaspoon xanthan gum

¼ cup erythritol

25 drops liquid stevia

1 tablespoon bourbon

Directions:

Melt the butter in a skillet over medium heat.

Add the pecans and season with salt. Reduce the heat to low and stir occasionally until the butter begins to turn a golden brown color, in approximately 5 minutes remove from the heat and let cool.

Using an immersion blender, combine the ricotta cheese, cooked pumpkin, cinnamon, coriander, coconut milk, egg yolks, xanthan gum, erythritol, liquid stevia and bourbon. Blend until smooth.

Transfer the mixture, along with the butter and pecans to an ice cream maker. Proceed according to manufacturer's instructions.

Maple and Buttered Coconut Ice Cream

Serves: 6

Net Carbs: 1.6 g

Nutritional Information: Calories 127.1, Total Fat 13.3 g, Total Carbohydrate 2.4 g, Dietary Fiber 0.8 g, Sugars 0.3 g, Protein 1.0 g

Ingredients:

1 cup full almond milk

¼ cup heavy whipping cream

¼ cup sour cream

2 teaspoons maple extract

20 drops liquid stevia

½ teaspoons xanthan gum

½ cup unsweetened, shredded coconut

2 tablespoon butter

½ teaspoon salt

Directions:

Place the almond milk heavy whipping cream, sour cream, maple extract, liquid stevia and xanthan gum in a container for use with an immersion blender.

Using the immersion blender, blend until creamy.

Melt the butter in a skillet over medium heat.

Add in the coconut and salt. Cook, stirring constantly for 3-4 minutes.

Remove the coconut from the heat and add to the rest of the mixture.

Use the immersion blender once more to fully incorporate the coconut.

Pour the mixture into an ice cream maker and proceed according to manufacturer's instructions.

Raspberry Almond Cheesecake Ice Cream

Serves: 6

Net Carbs: 5.1 g

Nutritional Information: Calories 357.5, Total Fat 33.9 g, Total Carbohydrate 9.7 g, Dietary Fiber 4.6 g, Sugars 2.6 g, Protein 8.6 g

Ingredients:

1½ cup full fat coconut milk

½ cup heavy cream

¼ cup erythritol

½ cup almond butter

1 cup cream cheese

1 teaspoon vanilla extract

1 teaspoon cinnamon

¼ teaspoon xanthan gum

1 cup raspberries

½ cup almonds, chopped

Directions:

Place the coconut milk and heavy cream in a saucepan over low heat.

Once the liquid is warmed through, add in the erythritol and stir until dissolved. Remove the pan from the heat.

In a blender combine the liquid with the almond butter, cream cheese, vanilla extract, cinnamon and xanthan gum. Blend well.

Fold in the raspberries and almonds.

Add the mixture to an ice cream maker and proceed according to manufacturer's instructions.

Ultimate Vanilla Ice Cream

Serves: 6

Net Carbs: 1.4 g

Nutritional Information: Calories 310.6, Total Fat 33.7 g, Total Carbohydrate 1.4 g, Dietary Fiber 0.0 g, Sugars 0.1 g, Protein 2.2 g

Ingredients:

1 cup heavy whipping cream

¼ cup erythritol

3 egg yolks

¼ cup butter, softened

¼ cup coconut oil

2 vanilla beans, scrapped

2 teaspoons pure vanilla extract

½ teaspoon salt

Directions:

Place the heavy whipping cream in a saucepan over low heat.

Once the cream is warm, add the erythritol and stir until dissolved.

Place the egg yolks in a bowl and add ¼ cup of the cream mixture to the bowl, whisking constantly to temper the eggs.

Slowly add the remaining cream, whisking constantly.

Place the egg mixture in a blender or food processor along with the butter, coconut oil, vanilla bean, vanilla extract and salt. Blend until creamy.

Transfer to an ice cream maker and proceed according to manufacturer's instructions.

Pumpkin Pie Ice Cream

Serves: 6

Net Carbs: 2.8 g

Nutritional Information: Calories 318.3, Total Fat 32.8 g, Total Carbohydrate 4.1 g, Dietary Fiber 1.3 g, Sugars 0.8 g, Protein 2.9 g

Ingredients:

1 cup pumpkin, cooked and pureed

¼ cup butter, softened

¼ cup coconut oil

½ cup heavy cream

3 egg yolks

20 drops liquid stevia

1 teaspoon vanilla extract

½ teaspoon maple extract

1 tablespoon pumpkin pie spice

1 tablespoon bourbon

½ cup pecans, chopped

Directions:

Combine the pumpkin, butter and coconut oil with a mixer until creamy.

Add in the heavy cream, eggs, liquid stevia, vanilla extract, maple extract, pumpkin pie spice and bourbon. Mix until blended and creamy.

Stir in the pecans. Transfer the mixture to an ice cream maker and proceed according to manufacturer's instructions.

Lemon Poppy Seed Ice Cream

Serves: 6

Net Carbs: 3.3 g

Nutritional Information: Calories 214.3, Total Fat 22.2 g, Total Carbohydrate 3.7 g, Dietary Fiber 0.4 g, Sugars 0.6 g, Protein 1.8 g

Ingredients:

2 cups full fat coconut milk

1 cup heavy whipping cream

½ cup lemon juice

1 tablespoon lemon zest

1 tablespoon poppy seeds

2 egg yolks

2 tablespoons coconut oil

1 teaspoon vanilla extract

20 drops liquid stevia

¼ teaspoon xanthan gum

Directions:

In a blender combine the coconut milk, heavy whipping cream, and lemon juice. Blend until creamy and thickened.

Add in the lemon zest, poppy seeds, egg yolks, coconut oil, vanilla extract, liquid stevia and xanthan gum. Blend until creamy.

Transfer the mixture to an ice cream maker and proceed according to manufacturer's instructions.

Mojito Ice Cream

Serves: 6

Net Carbs: 3.3 g

Nutritional Information: Calories 180.6, Total Fat 17.7 g, Total Carbohydrate 3.7 g, Dietary Fiber 0.4 g, Sugars 0.6 g, Protein 1.8 g

Ingredients:

2 cups full fat coconut milk

1 cup heavy whipping cream

2 egg yolks

½ cup lime juice

2 teaspoons lime zest

½ teaspoon vanilla extract

1 tablespoon rum

25 drops liquid stevia

¼ teaspoon xanthan gum

¼ cup fresh mint, chopped

Directions:

Combine the coconut milk, heavy whipping cream and egg yolks in a blender and blend until creamy and frothy.

Add in the lime juice, lime zest, vanilla extract, rum, liquid stevia, xanthan gum and mint. Blend until combined.

Pour the mixture into an ice cream maker and proceed according to manufacturer's instructions.

Chocolate Pistachio Ice Cream

Serves: 6

Net Carbs: 4.8 g

Nutritional Information: Calories 180.6, Total Fat 15.2 g, Total Carbohydrate 9.9 g, Dietary Fiber 5.1 g, Sugars 1.7 g, Protein 5.1 g

Ingredients:

2 cups full fat coconut milk

¼ cup erythritol

1 avocado, cubed

1 teaspoon vanilla extract

2 tablespoons dark cocoa powder

1 cup pistachios, chopped

Directions:

Place the coconut milk in a saucepan over medium low heat.

Once the milk is warmed, add the erythritol and stir until completely dissolved.

Remove from the heat, let cool and transfer to a blender.

Add in the avocado, vanilla extract, and dark cocoa powder. Blend until combined.

Stir in the pistachios.

Transfer the mixture to an ice cream machine and proceed according to manufacturer's instructions.

Extra Creamy Hazelnut Coffee Ice Cream

Serves: 6

Net Carbs: 2 g

Nutritional Information: Calories 194.9, Total Fat 19.8 g, Total Carbohydrate 3.2 g, Dietary Fiber 1.2 g, Sugars 0.9 g, Protein 2.3 g

Ingredients:

1 ½ cups full fat coconut milk

½ cup heavy whipping cream

½ cup crème fraiche

½ cup brewed espresso

1 vanilla bean, scrapped

1 teaspoon hazelnut extract

20 drops liquid stevia

½ cup hazelnuts, chopped

Directions:

Place the coconut milk, heavy whipping cream and crème fraiche in a container suitable for an immersion blender.

Using an immersion blender, blend the ingredients until smooth and slightly thickened.

Add in the espresso, vanilla bean, hazelnut extract, and liquid stevia. Blend until combined.

Stir in the hazelnuts.

Transfer the mixture to an ice cream maker and proceed according to manufacturer's instructions.

FROZEN TREATS
ON A STICK

Strawberry Lime Popsicles

Serves: 6

Net Carbs: 2.0 g

Nutritional Information: Calories 69.8, Total Fat 6.5 g, Total Carbohydrate 2.8 g, Dietary Fiber 0.8 g, Sugars 1.3 g, Protein 0.7 g

Ingredients:

¼ cup heavy cream

¼ cup sour cream

1 cup full fat coconut milk

1 cup strawberries

1 tablespoon lime juice

10 drops liquid stevia, or more to taste

Directions:

Place the strawberries in a blender and pulse until liquefied. If desired, strain the strawberries to remove any seeds and then transfer the mixture back into the blender.

Add in the heavy cream, sour cream, coconut milk, lime juice and liquid stevia. Continue to blend until creamy and slightly thickened.

Pour the mixture into popsicle molds and freeze for at least 4 hours before serving.

Orange Creamsicles

Serves: 6

Net Carbs: 2.9 g

Nutritional Information: Calories 285.9, Total Fat 30.5 g, Total Carbohydrate 2.9 g, Dietary Fiber 0.0 g, Sugars 1.6 g, Protein 2.3 g

Ingredients:

1 cup heavy whipping cream

½ cup cream cheese

¼ cup coconut oil

¼ cup orange juice

1 teaspoon orange extract

1 teaspoon vanilla extract

10 drops liquid stevia

Directions:

Place all of the ingredients in a container that can be used with an immersion blender.

Using the immersion blender, blend until creamy. Pour the mixture into popsicle molds.

Place in the freezer for at least 4 hours before serving.

Minty Cantaloupe Pops

Serves: 6

Net Carbs: 3.2 g

Nutritional Information: Calories 29.3, Total Fat 1.5 g, Total Carbohydrate 3.7 g, Dietary Fiber 0.5 g, Sugars 1.0 g, Protein 0.9 g

Ingredients:

1 cup cantaloupe, cubed

¼ cup water

1 cup coconut milk

½ cup plain full fat yogurt

10 drops liquid stevia

1 teaspoon vanilla extract

1 tablespoon fresh mint, finely chopped

Directions:

Place the cantaloupe and water in a blender and blend until liquefied.

Pour the cantaloupe equally into each of the popsicle molds.

Place the coconut milk, yogurt, liquid stevia, vanilla extract and mint in the blender and blend until combined.

Carefully pour that mixture into the popsicle molds over the cantaloupe layer.

Place in the freezer for at least 4 hours before serving.

Raspberry Forest Bars

Serves: 6

Net Carbs: 2.7 g

Nutritional Information: Calories 94.9, Total Fat 8.0 g, Total Carbohydrate 7.7 g, Dietary Fiber 5.0 g, Sugars 0.3 g, Protein 1.4 g

Ingredients:

2 cups full fat coconut milk, divided

1 cup raspberries

1 avocado, cubed

¼ cup dark cocoa powder

1 teaspoon vanilla extract

20 drops liquid stevia

¼ cup unsweetened, shredded coconut

Directions:

Combine 1 cup of the coconut milk and the raspberries in a blender. Blend until the raspberries have liquefied. Strain the mixture to remove the raspberry seeds, if desired.

Pour equal amounts of the raspberry mixture into the bottom of the popsicle molds.

Add the remaining coconut milk, avocado, cocoa powder, vanilla extract and liquid stevia to the blender and pulse until smooth.

Pour that mixture into the molds over the raspberry layer.

Sprinkle the shredded coconut over the bottom of the popsicles.

Place them in the freezer for at least 4 hours before serving.

Spicy Peach Layer Bars

Serves: 6

Net Carbs: 4.3 g

Nutritional Information: Calories 88.4, Total Fat 7.5 g, Total Carbohydrate 5.1 g, Dietary Fiber 0.8 g, Sugars 3.4 g, Protein 1.7 g

Ingredients:

1 cup frozen peach slices

¼ cup lime juice

¼ teaspoon cayenne pepper powder

¼ teaspoon cinnamon

1 cup full fat coconut milk

½ cup cream cheese

1 tablespoon lime zest

1 teaspoon vanilla extract

10 drops liquid stevia

Directions:

Place the frozen peaches, lime juice, cinnamon and cayenne pepper in a blender and pulse until liquefied.

Pour half of the mixture evenly into each of the molds and then place the molds in the freezer for 15 minutes. Set aside the remaining peach mixture.

In a blender combine the coconut milk, cream cheese, lime zest, vanilla extract and liquid stevia. Blend until smooth.

Remove the popsicles from the freezer and add the cream mixture to each of the molds.

Place the molds in the freezer for 15 minutes.

Remove the molds from the freezer and add the remaining peach mixture.

Place the molds back in the freezer for at least 4 hours before serving.

Creamy Fudgesicles

Serves: 6

Net Carbs: 2.3 g

Nutritional Information: Calories 146.7, Total Fat 14.6 g, Total Carbohydrate 3.5 g, Dietary Fiber 1.2 g, Sugars 1.2 g, Protein 3.4 g

Ingredients:

1 ¼ cup full fat coconut milk

1 teaspoon plain gelatin

1 cup cream cheese, softened

¼ cup dark cocoa powder

½ teaspoon nutmeg

1 teaspoon vanilla extract

20 drops liquid stevia

Directions:

Place the coconut milk in a saucepan and heat over medium.

Once the coconut milk is warmed through and steamy, add the gelatin and stir gently until dissolved. Remove from the heat and let cool slightly.

In a bowl combine the cream cheese, cocoa powder, nutmeg, vanilla extract and liquid stevia.

Pour the coconut milk mixture over the contents in the bowl.

Using an electric mixer, blend until creamy and thick.

Pour the mixture into popsicle molds.

Place the molds in the freezer for at least 4 hours before serving.

Raspberry Latte Bars

Serves: 6

Net Carbs: 1.0 g

Nutritional Information: Calories 73.8, Total Fat 6.5 g, Total Carbohydrate 2.5 g, Dietary Fiber 1.5 g, Sugars 0.0 g, Protein 0.2 g

Ingredients:

½ cup coconut milk

½ cup mascarpone cheese

½ cup brewed espresso

1 teaspoon vanilla extract

1 cup raspberries, chopped

20 drops liquid stevia

Directions:

Place the coconut milk, mascarpone cheese, espresso and vanilla extract in a blender and blend until creamy.

Pour the mixture into a bowl and stir in the raspberries and the liquid stevia.

Place the bowl in the freezer for 15-20 minutes, or until it begins to thicken and hold the raspberries in place when stirred.

Remove the bowl from the freezer and transfer the mixture to popsicle molds.

Place the molds in the freezer for at least 4 hours before serving.

Creamy Peanut Butter Popsicles

Serves: 6

Net Carbs: 4.2 g

Nutritional Information: Calories 181.2, Total Fat 13.8 g, Total Carbohydrate 6.0 g, Dietary Fiber 1.8 g, Sugars 1.7 g, Protein 6.7 g

Ingredients:

1 ½ cups full fat coconut milk

½ cup full fat plain yogurt

¾ cup natural peanut butter

10 drops liquid stevia

Directions:

Place all of the ingredients in a blender and blend until creamy.

Pour the mixture into popsicle molds.

Place the molds in the freezer for at least 4 hours before serving.

Cannoli Popsicles

Serves: 6

Net Carbs: 3.6 g

Nutritional Information: Calories 203.4, Total Fat 19.5 g, Total Carbohydrate 4.1 g, Dietary Fiber 0.5 g, Sugars 1.8 g, Protein 3.6 g

Ingredients:

1 cup heavy cream

½ cup ricotta cheese

½ cup almond milk

1 vanilla bean, scrapped

1 teaspoon cinnamon

¼ cup dark chocolate, chopped

Directions:

Place the heavy cream in a bowl and mix on high with an electric mixer until the cream begins to thicken.

Add in the ricotta cheese, almond milk, vanilla, cinnamon and chocolate.

Using the electric mixer, blend again until the mixture is smooth and creamy.

Spoon the mixture into popsicle molds.

Place them in the freezer for at least 4 hours before serving.

Cranberry Hazelnut Power Pops

Serves: 6

Net Carbs: 6.0 g

Nutritional Information: Calories 198.2, Total Fat 17.0 g, Total Carbohydrate 9.1 g, Dietary Fiber 3.1 g, Sugars 4.4 g, Protein 3.7 g

Ingredients:

1½ cup almond milk

½ cup mascarpone cheese

¼ cup almond butter

10 drops liquid stevia

1 teaspoon hazelnut extract

½ cup hazelnuts, chopped

¼ cup dried cranberries

1 tablespoon chia seeds

Directions:

Combine the almond milk, mascarpone cheese, almond butter, liquid stevia and hazelnut extract in a blender. Blend until creamy.

Stir in the hazelnuts, cranberries and chia seeds.

Spoon the mixture into popsicle molds.

Place the molds in the freezer and freeze for at least 4 hours before serving.

ketogenic
FROZEN
PIES

Strawberry and Peaches Pie

Serves: 8

Net Carbs: 5.5 g

Nutritional Information: Calories 408.1, Total Fat 41.8 g, Total Carbohydrate 7.9 g, Dietary Fiber 2.4 g, Sugars 3.3 g, Protein 5.7 g

Ingredients:

1 cup walnuts, chopped

1 cup unsweetened, shredded coconut

¼ cup erythritol

¼ cup butter, melted

½ teaspoon salt

½ cup strawberries, chopped

½ cup peaches, chopped

1 cup cream cheese, softened

1 cup heavy whipping cream

2 teaspoons lemon juice

1 teaspoon vanilla extract

20 drops liquid stevia

Directions:

Prepare the crust by combining the walnuts, coconut and erythritol in a blender or food processor. Pulse until smooth.

Pour the crust mixture into a bowl and add the melted butter. Mix until the butter is worked in throughout the crust mixture.

Press the crust into the bottom of a standard size pie dish.

Place the strawberries and peaches together in a blender and blend until smooth.

Add the cream cheese to a large bowl, and using an electric mixer, mix until creamy.

Slowly add in the whipping cream, lemon juice, vanilla extract and liquid stevia, beating with an electric mixer the entire time, until fluffy.

Pour the pureed fruit mixture into the cream mixture and stir gently until incorporated.

Spoon the mixture into the pie dish over the prepared crust.

Place in the freezer for at least 4 hours before serving.

Death by Chocolate Pie

Serves: 8

Net Carbs: 6.5 g

Nutritional Information: Calories 481.8, Total Fat 46.7 g, Total Carbohydrate 12.0 g, Dietary Fiber 5.5 g, Sugars 2.9 g, Protein 10.6 g

Ingredients:

1½ cup almond flour

½ cup dark unsweetened cocoa powder, divided

½ cup powdered erythritol, divided

¼ cup butter, melted

1 cup heavy whipping cream

1 cup almond milk

¼ cup butter, cubed

½ cup dark chocolate, chopped

¼ cup brewed espresso

1 tablespoon rum

1 teaspoon vanilla extract

½ teaspoon cinnamon

3 pasteurized eggs

1 cup walnuts, chopped

Directions:

In a bowl combine the almond flour, ¼ cup dark cocoa powder, ¼ cup powdered erythritol and the melted butter. Blend until crumbly.

Press the mixture into the bottom of a standard size pie dish.

Place the heavy cream, almond milk and butter in a sauce pan over medium heat. Cook, stirring frequently until the mixture comes to a boil. Remove the saucepan from the heat.

Stir in the remaining erythritol, remaining dark cocoa, chopped dark chocolate, espresso, rum, vanilla extract and cinnamon. Mix well.

Next, add in the eggs, whisking until they are well blended.

Fold in the walnuts and then transfer the mixture to the prepared pie dish.

Place in the refrigerator for at least 4 hours before serving.

Serve garnished with additional whipping cream or powdered cocoa, if desired.

Coconut Blackberry Fluff Pie

Serves: 10

Net Carbs: 6.3 g

Nutritional Information: Calories 431.4, Total Fat 41.1 g, Total Carbohydrate 8.6 g, Dietary Fiber 2.3 g, Sugars 2.8 g, Protein 11.1 g

Ingredients:

½ cup sunflower seeds

½ cup walnuts, chopped

¼ cup butter, melted

1 ½ cup cream cheese, softened

2 cups ricotta cheese

1 cup heavy whipping cream

¼ cup powdered erythritol

½ cup unsweetened shredded coconut

1 teaspoon coconut extract

1 cup blackberries, crushed

Additional coconut for garnish, if desired

Directions:

Place the sunflower seeds and walnuts in a blender or food processor and pulse until crumbly.

Place the mixture in a bowl and add the melted butter. Mix until the butter is evenly worked in throughout.

Press the crust mixture into the bottom of a standard size pie dish.

Place the cream cheese and ricotta cheese in a bowl and cream together using an electric mixer.

Slowly add in the whipping cream, erythritol and coconut extract. Blend until creamy and thickened.

Stir in the coconut and the blackberries.

Transfer the mixture to the prepared pie dish and garnish with additional coconut, if desired.

Place in the freezer for at least 4 hours before serving.

Better Than a PB&J Sandwich Pie

Serves: 10

Net Carbs: 8.4 g

Nutritional Information: Calories 466.3, Total Fat 41.6 g, Total Carbohydrate 13.3 g, Dietary Fiber 4.9 g, Sugars 3.6 g, Protein 12.4 g

Ingredients:

1½ cup almond flour

½ cup dark unsweetened cocoa powder

¼ cup erythritol

¼ cup butter, melted

1 cup heavy cream

1 cup cream cheese, softened

20 drops liquid stevia

1 cup natural peanut butter

1 cup blueberries

Directions:

Combine the almond flour, dark cocoa powder, erythritol and melted butter in a bowl. Mix until crumbly.

Press the mixture into the bottom of a standard size pie dish.

Place the heavy cream in an electric mixer and blend until thickened and peaks form.

In another bowl combine the cream cheese and liquid stevia. Blend until creamy.

Take one half of the whipped cream mixture, one half of the cream cheese mixture and the peanut butter and combine them until creamy. Pour this mixture into the bottom of the prepared pie dish.

In another bowl combine the remaining ingredients and the blueberries. Use an electric mixer to break up the blueberries slightly as you mix them.

Spread this mixture on top of the peanut butter layer.

Place the pie in the freezer for at least 4 hours before serving.

ketogenic
FROZEN
DESSERT
BOMBS

Coconut Lime Bombs

Serves: 12

Net Carbs: 0.7 g

Nutritional Information: Calories 133.1, Total Fat 14.4 g, Total Carbohydrate 2.1 g, Dietary Fiber 1.4 g, Sugars 0.6 g, Protein 0.6 g

Ingredients:

½ cup coconut oil

½ cup coconut butter

2 tablespoons full fat coconut milk

2 tablespoons lime juice

¼ cup powdered erythritol

1 teaspoon vanilla extract

¼ cup shredded coconut

1 tablespoon lime zest

Directions:

Prepare 12 mini muffin tins with liners or use mini silicone molds.

Combine the coconut oil, coconut butter, coconut milk, lime juice, erythritol and vanilla extract in a blender and blend until smooth. The mixture might be thin, depending on how liquefied the coconut oil becomes.

Spoon the mixture into the molds.

Place the coconut and lime zest in a food processor or spice grinder and chop.

Sprinkle the coconut mixture liberally over the bombs.

Place them in the freezer for at least 4 hours before serving.

Blackberry Coconut Cheesecake Bombs

Serves: 12

Net Carbs: 1.9 g

Nutritional Information: Calories 119.9, Total Fat 12.1 g, Total Carbohydrate 2.7 g, Dietary Fiber 0.8 g, Sugars 1.5 g, Protein 1.6 g

Ingredients:

1 cup cream cheese, softened

¼ cup coconut oil

¼ cup powdered eryhtritol

1 teaspoon vanilla extract

1 cup blackberries

¼ cup unsweetened, shredded coconut

Directions:

Prepare 12 mini muffin tins with liners or use mini silicone molds.

Place the blackberries, erythritol and vanilla extract in a blender. Pulse until the black berries are crushed. Remove from the blender and strain out the seeds only if desired.

With the blackberries in the blender, add in the cream cheese and coconut oil. Blend until creamy.

Spoon the mixture into the molds and sprinkle the shredded coconut.

Place them in the freezer for at least 4 hours before serving.

Walnut Orange Bombs

Serves: 12

Net Carbs: 1.9 g

Nutritional Information: Calories 185.9, Total Fat 19.1 g, Total Carbohydrate 2.6 g, Dietary Fiber 0.7 g, Sugars 1.2 g, Protein 3.7 g

Ingredients:

1½ cup cream cheese, softened

½ cup full fat coconut milk

2 tablespoons coconut oil

¼ cup powdered erythritol

1 teaspoon orange extract

1 tablespoon orange zest

1 cup walnuts, chopped

Directions:

Prepare 12 mini muffin tins with liners or use mini silicone molds.

In a blender combine the cream cheese, coconut milk, coconut oil, erythritol and orange extract. Blend until creamy.

Add in the orange zest and walnuts. Mix until well blended.

Spoon the mixture into each of the prepared molds.

Place in the freezer for at least 4 hours before serving.

Blueberry Basil Bombs

Serves: 12

Net Carbs: 1.9 g

Nutritional Information: Calories 111.3, Total Fat 11.1 g, Total Carbohydrate 2.2 g, Dietary Fiber 0.3 g, Sugars 1.5 g, Protein 0.8 g

Ingredients:

½ cup cream cheese, softened

½ cup mascarpone cheese

½ cup whole fat coconut milk

¼ cup powder erythritol

¼ cup coconut oil

1 teaspoon vanilla extract

1 tablespoon lemon zest

1 cup blueberries

¼ cup fresh basil, chopped

Directions:

Prepare 12 mini muffin tins with liners or use mini silicone molds.

In a blender combine the cream cheese, mascarpone cheese, coconut milk, erythritol and coconut oil. Blend until creamy.

Remove approximately one half of the mixture from the blender and set aside.

To the mixture still in the blender, add the lemon zest and blueberries. Blend until smooth.

Spoon the mixture into each of the molds, smoothing it to fill out the edges.

Rinse out the blender and add the remaining cheese mixture to it.

Add in the vanilla extract and basil. Blend until creamy and add as a second layer to the blueberry layer already in the molds.

Place them in the freezer for at least 4 hours before serving.

Italian Dessert Bombs

Serves: 12

Net Carbs: 0.2 g

Nutritional Information: Calories 123.5, Total Fat 12.2 g, Total Carbohydrate 0.3 g, Dietary Fiber 0.1 g, Sugars 0.0 g, Protein 0.1 g

Ingredients:

1½ cup mascarpone cheese

¼ cup brewed espresso, chilled

¼ cup powdered erythritol

½ teaspoon vanilla extract

1 tablespoon dark rum

1 tablespoon dark cocoa powder

1 tablespoon orange zest

Directions:

Prepare 12 mini muffin tins with liners or use mini silicone molds.

In a blender combine the mascarpone cheese, espresso, vanilla extract, erythritol and dark rum. Blend until creamy.

Spoon the mixture into each of the mini molds.

Carefully sift the cocoa powder over each bomb and then top with a sprinkling of orange zest.

Place in the freezer for at least 4 hours before serving.

Minty Chocolate Bombs

Serves: 12

Net Carbs: 0.9 g

Nutritional Information: Calories 117.0, Total Fat 11.2 g, Total Carbohydrate 2.1 g, Dietary Fiber 1.2 g, Sugars 0.6 g, Protein 0.5 g

Ingredients:

1 avocado

1 cup mascarpone cheese

2 tablespoon fresh mint, very finely chopped

1 teaspoon peppermint extract

½ teaspoon vanilla extract

10 drops liquid stevia

¼ cup dark chocolate, finely chopped

Directions:

Prepare 12 mini muffin tins with liners or use 12 mini silicone molds.

Place the avocado, mascarpone cheese and mint in a blender and blend until smooth.

Add the peppermint extract, vanilla extract, stevia and dark chocolate. Mix until blended.

Scoop a rounded spoonful of each mixture and place it in the tin or mold.

Place them in the freezer for at least 4 hours before serving.

Butter Rum Bombs

Serves: 12

Net Carbs: 0.4 g

Nutritional Information: Calories 225.2, Total Fat 23.0 g, Total Carbohydrate 1.4 g, Dietary Fiber 1.0 g, Sugars 0.4 g, Protein 0.9 g

Ingredients:

1½ cup mascarpone cheese

¼ cup butter

1 cup pecans, chopped

½ teaspoon cinnamon

½ teaspoon salt

¼ cup powdered erythritol

1 teaspoon vanilla extract

1 tablespoon dark rum

Directions:

Prepare 12 mini muffin tins with liners or use mini silicone molds.

Melt the butter in a sauté pan over medium heat.

Add the pecans to the pan, along with the cinnamon and the salt. Reduce the heat to medium low and cook, stirring occasionally, for 5 minutes.

Remove from heat and set aside until the butter cools, but doesn't completely solidify.

Add the mascarpone cheese to a blender along with the erythritol, vanilla extract and rum. Blend until creamy.

Add in the pecans and the butter. Pulse again until the butter is evenly incorporated throughout the mixture.

Spoon the mixture into the molds.

Place them in the freezer for at least 4 hours before serving.

Decadent Salted Double Chocolate Bombs

Serves: 12

Net Carbs: 1.5 g

Nutritional Information: Calories 263.5, Total Fat 27.3 g, Total Carbohydrate 3.4 g, Dietary Fiber 1.9 g, Sugars 1.3 g, Protein 2.7 g

Ingredients:

½ cup plus one tablespoon heavy whipping cream

½ cup almond butter

½ cup mascarpone cheese

¼ cup butter, softened

½ cup coconut oil

1 teaspoon vanilla extract

2 tablespoons dark cocoa powder

¼ cup dark chocolate, chopped

1 tablespoon coarse sea salt

Directions:

Prepare 12 mini muffin tins with liners or use mini silicone molds.

Place the ½ cup of heavy whipping cream in a bowl and beat with an electric mixture until thick peaks form.

Place the almond butter, mascarpone cheese, butter, coconut oil, remaining heavy cream and cocoa powder in a blender. Blend until smooth.

Pour the mixture into the whipped cream and gently fold in.

Fold in the chocolate pieces.

Spoon the mixture into the molds and top with a sprinkling of sea salt.

Place them in the freezer for at least 4 hours before serving.

Maple Nut Bombs

Serves: 12

Net Carbs: 1.0 g

Nutritional Information: Calories 162.4, Total Fat 17.0 g, Total Carbohydrate 2.7 g, Dietary Fiber 1.7 g, Sugars 0.8 g, Protein 3.1 g

Ingredients:

½ cup almond butter

¼ cup butter

¼ cup coconut oil

¼ cup powdered erythritol

2 teaspoons maple extract

½ cup walnuts, chopped

Directions:

Prepare 12 mini muffin tins with liners or use mini silicone molds.

Place the almond butter, butter, coconut oil, erythritol and maple extract in a saucepan.

Heat over low heat, while stirring, just until smooth.

Remove the pan from the heat and add in the walnuts.

Spoon the mixture into the molds.

Place in the freezer for at least 4 hours before serving.

Conclusion

The biggest part of sticking to any diet is to make it a part of your permanent lifestyle. This is especially important for plans such as the ketogenic diet which are created to not only teach you a new way of eating and approaching nutrition, but also changing the way your body metabolizes and responds to food. Looking into the future and thinking about never letting your lips touch a sweet treat again is simply too much for most of us to tolerate. Now, there is no need to even let such a terrifying thought enter your mind.

The goal of this book has been to help you eat ketogenically for life, by providing you with an incredible selection of sweet, frozen treats to enjoy along with your keto lifestyle. The recipes are rich, creamy, decadent and perfect for a quick sweet snack or the most special of occasions. With this collection, we urge you to celebrate life rather than get stuck in a rut. With your renewed energy and health as a result of eating ketogenically, you truly have every reason to enjoy the sweeter things in life and that, without question, includes dessert.